Electric Eels

by Sara van Dyck

Lerner Publications Company • Minneapolis

The author is most grateful to James Albert, Ph.D., University of Louisiana, Lafayette; Peter Moller, Ph.D., Hunter College, CUNY; and Philip Stoddard, Ph.D., Florida International University; each of whom reviewed portions of the text and generously shared information and suggestions. She wishes to thank Caroline Arnold, Sherrill Kushner, Alexis O'Neill, Joann Rocklin, and Gretchen Woelfle for their thoughtful comments.

The images in this book are used with the permission of: © George Grall/National Geographic/Getty Images, p. 4; © Laura Westlund/Independent Picture Service, p. 5; © Dr. Will Crampton, pp. 6, 15, 17, 18, 19, 38, 39, 40, 41, 47, 48 (top); © Willem Kolvoort/ naturepl.com, p. 7; © Ann & Rob Simpson, p. 8; © John G. Shedd Aquarium, pp. 9, 12, 26, 27, 31, 43; © Amazon-Images/Alamy, p. 10; © D. R. Schrichte/SeaPics.com, pp. 11, 24, 29, 36; © NHPA/Mark Bowler, p. 13; © Phillip Colla/SeaPics.com, p. 14; © David Fleetham/ Visuals Unlimited, p. 16; © Nature's Images/Photo Researchers, Inc., p. 20; © Dr. Charles McRae/Visuals Unlimited, p. 21; © Mark Smith/Photo Researchers, Inc., p. 22; © Nicole Duplaix/Peter Arnold, Inc., p. 23; © Norbert Wu/Minden Pictures/Getty Images, p. 25; © Richard T. Nowitz/Photo Researchers, Inc., pp. 28, 46; Suzanne Bolduc © WCS, p. 30; © Masa Ushioda/SeaPics.com, p. 32; © BIOS/Bringard Denis/Peter Arnold, Inc, p. 33; © Wim van Egmond/Visuals Unlimited, p. 34; © G. Czepluch/Peter Arnold, Inc., p. 35; © David Wrobel/Visuals Unlimited, p. 37; © Noel R. Kemp/Photo Researchers, Inc., p. 42; © Ken Lucas/Visuals Unlimited, p. 48 (bottom).

Front Cover: © Norbert Wu/Minden Pictures/Getty Images.

Copyright ©2008 by Lerner Publishing Group, Inc.

Lerner Publications Company
A division of Lerner Publishing Group, Inc.
241 First Avenue North
Minneapolis, Minnesota 55401 U.S.A.

Website address: www.lernerbooks.com

Library of Congress Cataloging-in-Publication Data

Van Dyck, Sara.
    Electric eels / by Sara van Dyck.
      p.   cm. — (Early bird nature books)
    Includes index.
    ISBN 978–0–8225–7886–4 (lib. bdg. : alk. paper)
    1. Electric eel—Juvenile literature. I. Title.
QL638.E34V36 2008
597'.48—dc22   2007023939

Manufactured in the United States of America
1 2 3 4 5 6 – JR – 13 12 11 10 09 08

Contents

Electric eels live in South America. The striped areas on this map show exactly where electric eels live.

Be a Word Detective

Can you find these words as you read about electric eels?
Be a detective and try to figure out what they mean.
You can turn to the glossary on page 46 for help.

dams   freshwater   oxygen
electric organs   gills   predators
electroreceptors   insulation cells   prey
fins   larvas

There is more than one way to form plurals of some words.
The word larva *has two possible plural endings—either an*
e or an s. *In this book,* s *is used when many larvas are*
being discussed.

Chapter 1

South America has many rivers and streams. What kind of fish lives in the streams?

A Fish That Shocks

A powerful fish swims in the streams of South America. This fish is called the electric eel. People do not see it often. But they may feel it when they step into the water. Zap! The

fish sends out an electric shock. That hurts.
The people jump out of the water fast.

The electric eel's scientific name is Electrophorus electricus.

The skin under an electric eel's body is yellowish gray.

The electric eel looks like a thick snake.
It has a wide head. Its body is brown and dark
gray, with yellow underneath. Its skin is thick
and smooth.

An electric eel can grow to be 8 feet long. That's twice as long as a broomstick. An electric eel is about as big around as your leg.

An adult electric eel weighs about 45 pounds. That's about as much as a first grader weighs.

An electric eel has two small fins behind its head. One fin is on each side of the fish's body.

Fish have fins. Fins are parts of the body that help fish swim. The electric eel has three fins. It has a pair of short fins behind its head.

The electric eel uses these fins to steer as it swims. It also has one long fin under its body. This fin helps the electric eel swim backward and forward.

An electric eel has a long fin under its body. The fin starts behind the fish's head and ends at the tip of its tail.

The electric eel does not have ears that stick out like ours. But it can hear very well. It can hear other animals moving in the water.

An electric eel has ears, but they do not stick out the way people's ears do.

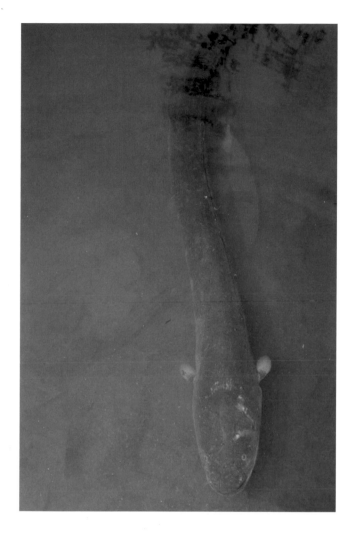

This electric eel lives in water that is hard to see through.

Electric eels have small eyes. They are blue or green. Electric eels cannot see well. But they do not need to see much. They live in muddy water that is hard to see through. And they hunt for food at night, when it is too dark to see.

All animals need to breathe oxygen (AHKS-uh-jihn) to live. Oxygen is a gas. It is in the air and in water. You breathe oxygen into your lungs. Fish don't have lungs. Instead, they have gills. Fish use their gills to take oxygen from the water.

An electric eel's gills are in front of its small fins.

The electric eel's gills take in some oxygen. But the water electric eels live in does not have much oxygen. So every few minutes, an electric eel swims to the top of the water. Then it gulps air into its mouth. It gets more oxygen from the air.

This electric eel is coming to the top of the water to breathe. If an electric eel stays underwater for more than 15 minutes, it will drown.

Fishes called true eels look a lot like electric eels. But true eels and electric eels are not the same. True eels have fins on their backs. And true eels are born in salty oceans. Electric eels do not have back fins. They live in freshwater all their lives. Freshwater is water that is not salty.

Moray eels are true eels. They have a long fin on their backs.

This is one kind of knifefish that lives in South America. Its scientific name is Eigenmannia limbata.

Knifefishes are relatives of the electric eel. Knifefishes can make electricity. But they can't make as much electricity as electric eels can.

Chapter 2

Some electric eels live in shallow streams in the rain forest. What are some other places electric eels live?

Danger in the Water

 The electric eel lives near the Amazon River in South America. It lives in the shallow

water of streams, ponds, swamps, and lakes.
The electric eel often hides among water plants.

Giant water lilies grow in shallow water near the Amazon River. They have round, floating leaves that are more than 6 feet wide. Their flowers are as big as soccer balls!

Piranhas (puh-RAHN-uhz) aren't big. But these fish have very sharp teeth. Groups of piranhas hunt together. They can kill large animals.

Electric eels are predators (PREH-duh-turz). Predators are animals that kill and eat other animals. The electric eel shares the water with other fierce predators. It lives with stingrays, piranhas, anaconda (AN-uh-KAHN-duh) snakes, and caimans (KAY-muhnz). Caimans are relatives of alligators.

Electric eels are top predators. That means other animals do not hunt them. Electric eels are too dangerous!

This caiman is eating a big fish.

The electric eel hunts crabs and fish. It also eats young insects that live in the water. The animals the electric eel hunts are called its prey.

Many different kinds of catfish live in South America.

Usually electric eels get along with one another.

Electric eels are friendly to one another most of the time. In the Amazon, they often swim together in the shallow water. But if too many electric eels are crowded together, they may fight. They may bite one another. They may slap one another's tails. Or they may zap one another with electricity.

Chapter 3

Adult electric eels can't see well. How do they find out about their world?

Zap! Zap!

You use your eyes to find out what is going on. Dogs use their noses. But the electric eel does not see or smell well. Instead, it uses electricity to learn about its world.

More than 100 kinds of fish make electricity. Some electric fishes live in rivers in South America and Africa. Others live in the ocean. The electric eel is the most powerful of all electric fishes.

Electric rays are fish with round, flat bodies. Some of them can make strong electric shocks.

The electric eel's heart and other body parts are packed into the front of its body. Electric organs fill most of its long tail.

The parts of the electric eel's body that make electricity are called electric organs. Each electric eel has three pairs of electric organs. They are inside the eel's long tail. One pair of electric organs is short. The other two pairs are longer.

Organs are made up of cells. Different kinds of cells do different jobs. The cells in the eel's electric organs make electricity. Each electric organ is made up of thousands of cells. It's like having thousands of tiny batteries hooked together.

The electric eel can feel electricity too. The eel has cells called electroreceptors (ih-LEHK-tro-rih-SEHP-terz). The electroreceptors are in the eel's skin. They pick up electrical signals from the water.

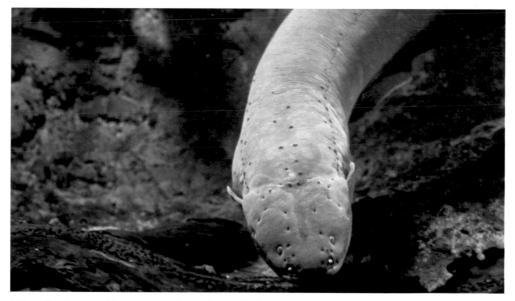

The dark marks on an electric eel's head and body are pores. Pores are small holes in the skin. The pores help the electric eel pick up electrical signals from the water.

When an electric eel is swimming, its short electric organs make weak bursts of electricity. These bursts of electricity help the eel find out what is around it. They tell the eel if other fish are nearby. They may also send messages to other electric eels.

An electric eel uses electricity to find its way around objects in the water.

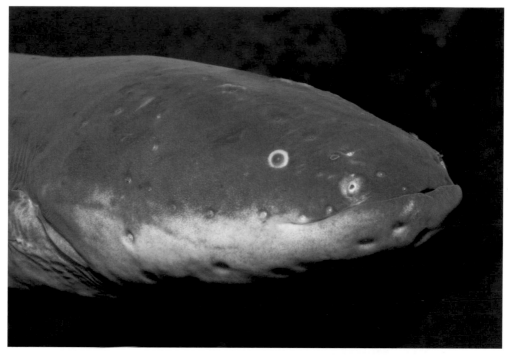

The electric eel has a wide mouth. It swallows its food whole.

When an electric eel finds prey, the eel's long electric organs act quickly. They make many strong bursts of electricity. These bursts knock out the prey. The eel swallows the prey in one gulp.

The electric eel also uses electricity to keep itself safe. If another predator gets too close, the eel makes strong bursts of electricity. The bursts hurt or kill the other animal.

A small electric eel can make only a little electricity. A bigger fish can make much stronger shocks. Its electricity can light up a lightbulb! An adult electric eel can make enough electricity to kill a small animal.

Small electric eels use their electricity to knock out small animals. Bigger electric eels can make enough electricity to kill animals.

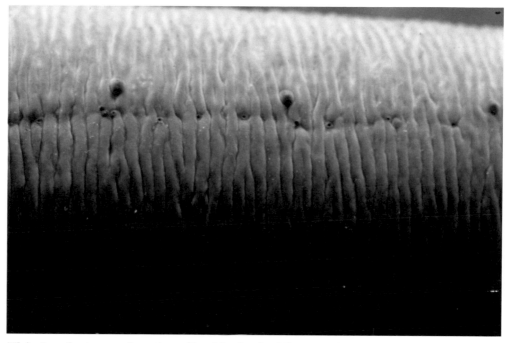

This is what an electric eel's skin looks like up close.

Usually an electric eel is not hurt by its own electricity. The eel has special cells in its skin. The cells are called insulation (IHN-suh-LAY-shuhn) cells. Insulation cells protect the eel from shocks.

Sometimes an electric eel's skin gets scratched or cut. Then the eel's insulation may not work well. If the electric eel makes electricity, it may shock itself.

Chapter 4

Electric eels hatch from eggs. Where do electric eels lay their eggs?

Mom, Dad, and Hundreds of Kids

When a female electric eel is ready to lay eggs, the male electric eel builds a nest in the water. The nest is made of air bubbles. The male hides the nest in some water plants.

The female electric eel lays hundreds of eggs in the bubble nest. Baby electric eels will hatch from the eggs. If the eggs sink, the baby eels will drown. The bubbles help the eggs float in the water.

The male stays near the eggs. He keeps other animals from eating them. One week later, baby eels begin to hatch from the eggs. The newly hatched eels are called larvas.

Different kinds of fish make bubble nests. This bubble nest was made by a Siamese fighting fish. The white dots in the nest are eggs. The bubbles help the eggs float.

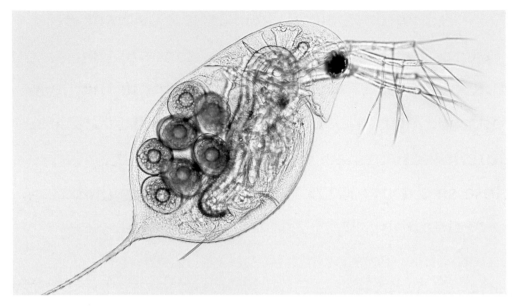

Electric eel larvas eat tiny animals. Many tiny animals live in South America's streams and lakes. This animal is a daphnia.

The male eel guards the larvas. The larvas are very small. But they can make a little bit of electricity. The larvas eat eggs that have not hatched yet. They also eat tiny creatures in the water.

Soon the larvas are about 3 inches long. They are longer than your fingers. By this time, the larvas can eat larger creatures. They eat baby shrimp and other kinds of foods.

The young electric eels stay close to their parents. Sometimes they swim close to their parents' heads. Scientists do not know why the larvas do this. Maybe they stay close so their parents can protect them. Or maybe they stay close so they can use electricity to send messages to their parents.

As young electric eels grow larger, they can eat bigger food such as small fish. Neon tetras are small fish that live in South America.

The young electric eels grow bigger. They make stronger and stronger electric shocks. Soon they begin to use their electricity to kill prey. When they are about one year old, they leave their parents. They are big enough to live by themselves.

An electric eel can live for 10 to 20 years.

An adult electric eel's eyes can't see much. The eel uses electricity to find out what is around it.

An electric eel's skin has insulation cells. Its eyes don't have these cells. When an electric eel is young, it can see. But each time the eel makes a burst of electricity, the shock harms its eyes. An adult electric eel is almost blind. But it can still tell what is around it. The eel is still a powerful hunter.

Chapter 5

People live along the rivers and streams where electric eels live. Why did some people catch electric eels long ago?

Hard to Catch

Long ago, people in South America caught electric eels. They used the eels to try to make sick people well. They thought the eels' electricity could help people with headaches or fevers.

In modern times, scientists catch electric eels. They want to study the fish. Scientists catch the eels in big nets. The scientists must wear heavy rubber boots and gloves. Rubber is a kind of insulation. It helps to protect the scientists from electricity. But when the scientists get in the water with an electric eel, they still feel the eel's shocks!

This scientist is getting ready to look for electric eels.

These scientists are measuring an electric eel that they caught. They are wearing rubber gloves so they won't be shocked.

At first, an electric eel sends out many strong bursts of electricity. After a while, it does not have as much energy. It's as though its batteries have run down. The eel can still make weak shocks. But they are so weak that people can easily catch the eel.

Scientists have used electric eels to study electricity. They also use electric eels to learn how cells in our own bodies talk to one another.

Scientists hope electric eels can show us more about how our brains work.

People do not often hunt electric eels. But the eels still may not be safe. People who live in South America's rain forests catch fish that electric eels eat. If the people catch too many fish, electric eels may not have enough to eat.

People in South America drag big nets behind boats to catch fish.

Itaipu Dam is a huge dam on the Paraná River in South America.

In some places in South America, people want to build dams on the rivers. A dam is a wall built across a river. It keeps water from flowing. If dams are built, electric eels will not have as much water to live in.

Electric eels are amazing animals.

Electric eels can be scary creatures. But they are part of nature. They have lived on Earth for millions of years. They share the streams with catfish, turtles, and caimans. The electric eels belong in South America's waters.

A NOTE TO ADULTS
ON SHARING A BOOK

When you share a book with a child, you show that reading is important. To get the most out of the experience, read in a comfortable, quiet place. Turn off the television and limit other distractions, such as telephone calls.

Be prepared to start slowly. Take turns reading parts of this book. Stop occasionally and discuss what you're reading. Talk about the photographs. If the child begins to lose interest, stop reading. When you pick up the book again, revisit the parts you have already read.

BE A VOCABULARY DETECTIVE

The word list on page 5 contains words that are important in understanding the topic of this book. Be word detectives and search for the words as you read the book together. Talk about what the words mean and how they are used in the sentence. Do any of these words have more than one meaning? You will find the words defined in a glossary on page 46.

WHAT ABOUT QUESTIONS?

Use questions to make sure the child understands the information in this book. Here are some suggestions:

What did this paragraph tell us? What does this picture show? What do you think it's like being an electric eel? Where do electric eels live? How are electric eels different from true eels? How do electric eels breathe? What do electric eels eat? How do electric eels find out if other fish are nearby? Why doesn't an electric eel shock itself? What is your favorite part of the book? Why?

If the child has questions, don't hesitate to respond with questions of your own, such as What do *you* think? Why? What is it that you don't know? If the child can't remember certain facts, turn to the index.

INTRODUCING THE INDEX

The index helps readers find information without searching through the whole book. Turn to the index on page 48. Choose an entry such as *electricity* and ask the child to use the index to find out how electric eels use electricity. Repeat with as many entries as you like. Ask the child to point out the differences between an index and a glossary. (The index helps readers find information, while the glossary tells readers what words mean.)

ELECTRIC EELS

BOOKS

Arnold, Caroline. *Shockers of the Sea: And Other Electric Animals*. Watertown, MA: Charlesbridge Publishing, 1999. This book has information about other animals that make electricity.

Cast, C. Vance. *Where Does Electricity Come From?* Hauppauge, NY: Barron's Educational Series, 1992. Find out where the electricity in your wall sockets comes from.

Lovett, Sarah. *Extremely Weird Fishes*. Emeryville, CA: Avalon Travel Publishing, 1996. See different kinds of unusual fish close-up.

Walker, Sally M. *Electricity*. Minneapolis: Lerner Publications Company, 2006. This book has some simple experiments you can do with electricity.

WEBSITES

About Rainforests
http://ran.org/index.php?id=954
This site has a lot of information about rain forests, including a video, rain forest terms, fact sheets, and more.

Electric Eel
http://www.georgiaaquarium.org/animalguide/riverscout/electriceel.aspx
This website has lots of information about the electric eel.

Electricity by BrainPOP
http://www.brainpop.com/science/energy/electricity/
This website has a video that explains the different types of electricity and how they work.

Rainforest: What's It Like Where You Live?
http://www.mbgnet.net/sets/rforest/index.htm
This website looks at the two types of rain forests in the world, along with the plants and animals that live in them.

GLOSSARY

dams: walls built across rivers that keep water from flowing

electric organs: the parts of an electric eel's body that make electricity

electroreceptors (ih-LEHK-tro-rih-SEHP-terz): cells in an electric eel's skin that pick up electrical signals from the water

fins: parts of the body that help fish swim

freshwater: water that is not salty

gills: parts of a fish's body that take oxygen out of the water

insulation (IHN-suh-LAY-shuhn) cells: special cells in an electric eel's skin that protect the eel from electric shocks

larvas: newly hatched electric eels

oxygen (AHKS-uh-jihn): a gas that is found in the air and in water. All animals need to breathe oxygen.

predators (PREH-duh-turz): animals that kill and eat other animals

prey: animals that are hunted and eaten by other animals

INDEX

Pages listed in **bold** type refer to photographs.